THE
HAPPINESS
JOURNAL

THE
HAPPINESS
JOURNAL

Creative Activities
to Bring Joy to Your Day

MICHAEL O'MARA BOOKS LIMITED

First published in Great Britain in 2020
By Michael O'Mara Books Limited
9 Lion Yard
Tremadoc Road
London SW4 7NQ

A CIP catalogue record for this book is available from the British Library.

Papers used by Michael O'Mara Books Limited are natural, recyclable
products made from wood grown in sustainable forests. The manufacturing
processes conform to the environmental regulations of the country of origin.

ISBN: 978-1-78929-268-8 in paperback print format

Designed by Ana Bjezancevic

Illustrated by Carole Hénaff

Every reasonable effort has been made to acknowledge all copyright holders.
Any errors or omissions that may have occurred are inadvertent, and anyone
with any copyright queries is invited to write to the publisher, so that full
acknowledgement may be included in subsequent editions of the work.

Printed and bound in China

MIX
Paper from
responsible sources
FSC
www.fsc.org   FSC® C020056

THIS BOOK BELONGS TO:

zoe
wytrykowski

INTRODUCTION

We could all do with a bit more happiness in our lives,
whether that's the laugh-out-loud kind, the excited and
can't wait kind, or the state of quiet contentment kind. Of
course, no one can be blissfully happy all the time – we're
not meant to be and to strive for such a goal at the expense
of listening to what's really going on for us actually has the
opposite effect. But sometimes we can find ourselves feeling
out of balance, stuck and in need of some inspiration.

The exercises in this book aim to help you make space for the positives in your life and create more opportunities for happiness to grow. There's lots of room for you to record your own experiences, reflections and ideas, because what happiness means and how we build it into our lives is different for each of us. So, take your time, get creative and see what works for you.

ALL OF YOU IS WELCOME HERE

No one can be happy all of the time. We're not designed that way, no matter what our social media feeds might encourage us to believe. We come with the full spectrum of emotions for a good reason. However, we are often told that there are 'good' feelings and 'bad' feelings. And certainly some feelings can be uncomfortable or painful to experience. But the truth is that our feelings act as messengers about our experiences and if we just strive to feel happy all of the time, or judge ourselves when we're not, we can ignore how we're really feeling and that tends to have the opposite effect.

Try this mindfulness-based exercise to check in with how you're feeling right now.

● Sit comfortably in an upright position.

● Take a couple of slow, deep breaths,
then close your eyes.

● Breathe normally and place your attention on the movement
of air as you inhale and exhale.

● See if you can allow whatever feelings you are currently
experiencing to be with you right now – just as they are.

● Name each emotion that you are feeling.

● Accept that you are feeling this way. Remember that you don't
have to like it. Acceptance is about acknowledging that you
can't control how you are feeling and you don't need to.

● Recognize that these feelings are not trying
to hurt you and they will pass.

● Remind yourself that you are human and you
are allowed to feel your feelings.

● Whenever your mind wanders just notice that this has
happened and where it's gone to and then gently return your
attention to your breath and then back to your feelings.

● Try to maintain this focus for a few minutes.

● When you're ready to finish, open your eyes.

Take a moment to record here what the experience was like for you. And remember not to judge yourself if you found it tough.

Tip / Making this exercise a regular part of your routine can be a useful way of making space for your emotions and practising self acceptance.

The Good Stuff

Take a moment now to think of some of the good things in your life. It might be loved ones, an achievement that you're proud of or simply your cat's purr. Write down what comes to mind here. Focusing on the things that make us smile can help shift our perspective, promoting optimism and fostering positivity. But for many of us, it's all too easy to get wrapped up in our everyday struggles. Creating visual reminders is an effective way of keeping the good stuff close. These might be photos (in frames, stuck to your fridge, attached to your keyring) or they might be more symbolic, such as tickets from a brilliant gig or a souvenir from a special trip.

Think about when and where you might benefit from these reminders. It could be by your front door to greet you when you get in, on your desk at work or as your phone's background so you can carry it with you.

TIP/ We can often stop noticing things when they become familiar so don't forget to make new reminders now and again.

'You must be the best judge of your own happiness.'

Jane Austen

HAPPINESS IS . . .

Happiness can come in many forms, from moments of joy to a more lasting state of peace. It can be found in raucous laughter and quiet reflection, in memories of the past and anticipation of the future. Happiness can be exciting, comforting, expectant, satisfied and much, much more besides.

What does happiness mean to you? How do you experience happiness? What people, memories, objects, music, pictures, tastes, smells and sensations do you associate with happiness?

On the opposite page, scribble down as many ideas as you can. As a starting point, you could think about completing the sentence: 'Happiness is . . .'

HAPPINESS IS . . .

'These pains you
feel are messengers.
Listen to them.'

Rumi

WHAT DOES HAPPINESS LOOK LIKE?

How would you draw a picture of happiness? Would it be a person, a scene from memory, an object? Or perhaps something more abstract? What colours, shapes, patterns come to mind?

Try holding the idea of that happy image in your mind, and all that you associate with it, as you create a drawing here. It doesn't matter how messy or imperfect the results, it's the process that counts.

TIP/ Flip back to **'Happiness is . . .'** for some ideas on what you might draw.

Make it a Real Break

Busy day ahead? Schedule in some breaks and make
a plan for what you're going to do with them.

It might be an hour for lunch or a snatched five minutes
but, however you take time for yourself, make sure that
it's a proper break and you're not just idly scrolling
through your phone, or casting an eye over emails,
or being interrupted by family or colleagues.

Think about what helps you to recharge. It might be
enjoying a mug of something warming, finding a quiet place
to sit and letting your mind wander, listening to music or
getting outside for a short walk. You could do a breathing
exercise or draw or doodle or colour in this book.

Set a time frame for your break and stick to it
and, most importantly, give yourself conscious
permission to really relax. The rest can wait.

'Tension is who you think you should be. Relaxation is who you are.'

Chinese proverb

Give Yourself Permission

Many of us struggle at times to actually do the things that make us happy. We may feel that we don't have enough time or that we ought to be taking care of others before ourselves. We can label activities that bring us happiness as unnecessary, indulgent or even selfish. We'll do it later, or next week/month, when we're less busy. Maybe we'll get to it, but maybe we won't. As time goes on, our needs and our happiness can slip further down the scale of priorities.

But when we neglect our own happiness, we lose our sense of balance; stress and worry can build and we actually find it harder to manage those things we thought were more important. Because far from being selfish, finding time for the things that bring us happiness is a responsibility that we have not only to ourselves but also to those around us.

On the opposite page, write yourself a permission slip to remind yourself of this commitment. Include details of why it's important that you take this time for yourself and the benefits to you and those around you.

I GIVE MYSELF PERMISSION TO . . .

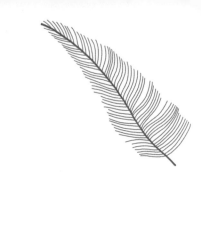

WHAT BRINGS YOU HAPPINESS?

Fill the opposite page with ideas for activities that will make you happy. These could be meeting up with friends, watching movies, taking a walk by yourself, painting, knitting, playing sports, anything that you *do* which brings you a sense of happiness.

For ideas, flip back to **'Happiness is . . .'** and think about all the different kinds of happiness represented by the things you listed. For instance, the happiness that makes you laugh out loud, that's just for fun, that makes your heart beat fast, that gives you that sense of purpose, that helps you feel relaxed and content. What activities help you to feel these different kinds of happiness?

'As soap is to the
body, so laughter
is to the soul.'

Yiddish proverb

Your Natural World

Being in nature – whether that's in the middle of the countryside, your garden or the local park (or even just looking at it through a window) – has been shown to have a powerful effect on our wellbeing, reducing stress and anxiety, and improving mood. The changes are felt throughout the body as our blood pressure drops and even our immune system gets a boost. We also enjoy a rise in the neurotransmitter serotonin, one of the body's feel-good chemicals.

When do you encounter nature in your daily life? The next time you leave your home, pay particular attention to what nature is around. Even in cities there will be trees lining the streets, mosses and small plants growing in the cracks of walls and bushes growing over garden walls. Stop and take a few minutes to get closer and focus in on the details. Check in with each of your senses: sight, touch, smell, hearing – although it's probably best to leave out taste for this one.

Next, give your mind time to appreciate some of the subtle and extraordinary intricacies of how that tree or plant lives, how it finds nutrients and light and the part it plays in its particular ecosystem. Think about how it provides shelter and food for insects, birds, fungi and other plants. Consider the parts that you can't see – the roots underground, the vessels inside the stems – and how they all operate together to support life.

You can also check in with the same plant or tree throughout the year and notice what changes take place as the seasons come and go.

TIP / Don't forget to look up. Whether it's day or night, the sky is something we always have access to and it is always changing. Let your eyes become accustomed to the light level (although never look directly at the sun) and just notice any colours, shapes and movement. Even on the greyest day there is variation in the clouds and, just like with our feelings, they will always move on.

'If you truly love
nature, you will find
beauty everywhere.'

Vincent van Gogh

POSITIVES LOG

Sometimes we need to take the time to pay attention to what's going well in our lives. It can be all too easy to listen out for the negatives, the criticism and the problems that need to be solved. But this often comes at the expense of the positives, the compliments and the successes. Without knowing it, we develop an inaccurate, one-sided story about how our day went and, if we repeat that same pattern day after day, it can change our life story and how we feel about ourselves.

Over the next week, make a conscious effort to notice the positives and keep a record of them here. It may be tricky at first – just as it is to change any habit – and you might miss things or feel like the negatives still outweigh the positives but, with practice, you'll likely notice more and more, the log will grow and it'll become a more natural way of thinking.

This isn't about trying to put a positive spin on tough times or bad experiences, or not allowing ourselves to feel low (see **'All of You is Welcome Here'** for more). Rather, it's about making sure that we aren't missing or dismissing the good things when they happen.

MONDAY

TUESDAY

WEDNESDAY

THURSDAY

FRIDAY

SATURDAY

SUNDAY

TIP/ Don't forget the small stuff. The 'thank you', the 'nice one'
– it all counts.

'To observe
attentively is to
remember distinctly.'

Edgar Allan Poe

CELEBRATE SUCCESSES

Look back at your positives log and highlight or circle all your accomplishments and successes. If you feel there aren't any, think back over what happened during the week – they will be there, even if at first you can't see them.

They might seem small, or they might feel crowded out by what you see as failures, but remembering to water the plants, finishing that piece of work, having that tough conversation, being on time for work (even if you were late on all the other days) all count as successes if you personally find them difficult.

Celebrate your successes. Congratulate yourself. Reward yourself. Choose one of the things in that list and write about it here. Think about why it was a challenge and what you did to overcome it. Allow yourself to feel pride in your achievement as you write.

THE POWER OF ANTICIPATION

You can squeeze even more happiness out of activities you enjoy if you give yourself the opportunity to look forward to them. Research has shown that anticipating things we enjoy can have a powerful, positive impact on our mood. So, block out the time in your diary, place sticky notes on your fridge, put reminders in your phone – whatever will help you to keep in mind the good things to come.

Don't just save this for the big events, such as holidays – spread the power of anticipation to the every day. Think about things like coffee breaks, time with friends or family, relaxing in front of the TV. During stressful times, being reminded that something we enjoy is just around the corner can be particularly helpful. And not only will you get a boost from thinking about what's to come, it'll also make you more likely to plan more lovely things to look forward to.

On the opposite page, write a list of things you enjoy doing that you could fit into the coming week. Note next to them when you'll do them and decide how you can build that sense of anticipation.

'Pleasure is found
first in anticipation,
later in memory.'

Gustave Flaubert

ONE POSITIVE CHANGE

Not everything that brings us happiness is easy or fun to do. Sometimes, it's about making a difficult change, breaking a habit or building a new one in order to gain the benefits.

Write down here, in big letters, one positive, realistic change that you would like to make in your life.

○ What small thing could you do today to get you closer to that goal? Note that down, too.

○ Now do it!

TIP / If you find it tough to make that first step, turn to **'What Holds You Back?'**.

'True life is lived when
tiny changes occur.'

Leo Tolstoy

WHAT HOLDS YOU BACK?

Whether it's being afraid of failure or that we won't do a good job, feeling like we don't have enough time or being overwhelmed by how big the task is, there are lots of ways in which we can feel held back from making positive changes in our lives.

Have a think now about what is holding you back from making a start. Write down what comes to mind below.

Now, turn your mind to what might start to make a difference. It could be about taking that really big job and breaking it down into manageable parts that you then tackle one at a time. It might be taking a hard look at your schedule and working out what you can shift around to make space. It might be about confronting your ideas of failure and reminding yourself that we all fail and it's OK – in fact, it's necessary, otherwise how would we ever learn? It might be about enlisting the help of family or friends. It might be deciding to seek professional help to talk through what's holding you back, such as a counsellor. It might be all of these things. Or it might be that, actually, upon deeper reflection, the thing that you thought you wanted, you don't really want after all.

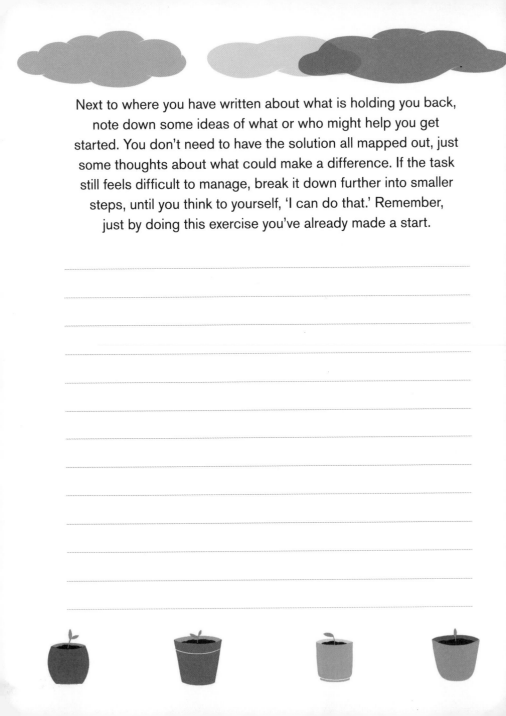

Next to where you have written about what is holding you back, note down some ideas of what or who might help you get started. You don't need to have the solution all mapped out, just some thoughts about what could make a difference. If the task still feels difficult to manage, break it down further into smaller steps, until you think to yourself, 'I can do that.' Remember, just by doing this exercise you've already made a start.

'The most difficult thing is the decision to act, the rest is merely tenacity.'

Amelia Earhart

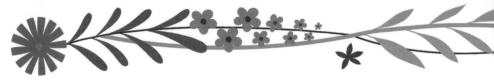

TOUGH TIMES

We will all go through tough times, and it's important to allow ourselves not to deny these experiences and feel like we have to bounce back before we are ready. However, that doesn't mean that you can't care for yourself through the struggles.

Some people have what's called a 'self-soothing box' where they keep items that bring them comfort and remind them of where they can find help if they need it.

Jot down some ideas of things that could go in your own self-soothing box.

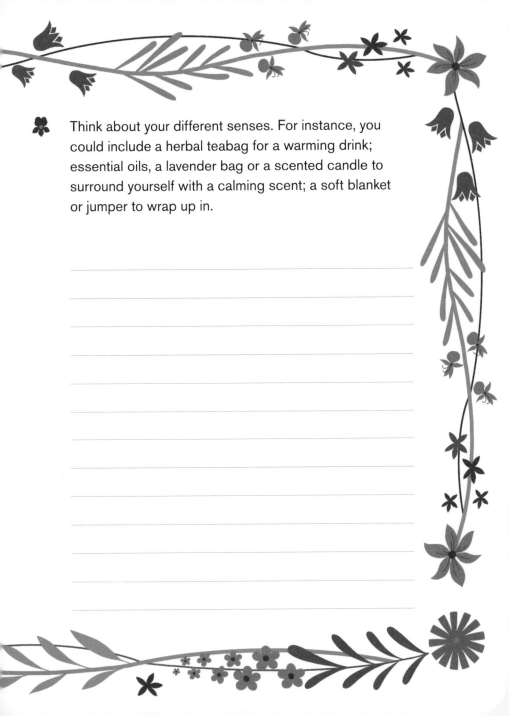

Think about your different senses. For instance, you could include a herbal teabag for a warming drink; essential oils, a lavender bag or a scented candle to surround yourself with a calming scent; a soft blanket or jumper to wrap up in.

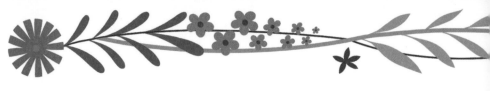

What books or films do you find familiar and reassuring?

Mementos that inspire positive emotions – such as photos, postcards and cards – can also be a big help.

✿ Don't forget to include the name and number of a trusted friend or family member who you can talk to. You could also include a reminder of other sources of help, such as useful websites or helplines.

_____

_____

_____

_____

_____

_____

✿ It might also be helpful to include a reminder of what to avoid, such as encouraging yourself to take a break from social media, or keeping an eye on drinking alcohol? Goes better with encouraging and staying in same sentence.

_____

_____

_____

Breathe in Relaxation

When you are relaxed your breathing automatically switches to a deeper, slower rhythm. It's one of the reasons why breathing is so important to meditation. And we can use this connection in reverse to help bring on that state of relaxation when we're feeling worked up or stressed.

We can bolster the physiological effects of breathing deeply by combining it with a mental process that also helps encourage us to relax. The exercise here uses a focus word to do this. What word you choose is entirely up to you, but the point is that it brings to mind the sensation of relaxation. Some people like to simply use the word 'relax' or 'breathe'.

TIP / Sometimes, when we're in a heightened state of emotion or anxiety deep breathing will not be enough to bring us into a relaxed state. Don't worry or judge yourself if this happens to you. Each of us is different and there may well be other techniques and approaches that will help. Talking with your doctor or a trained counsellor or therapist is a good way to find out more.

1. Sit or lie in a comfortable place.

2. Bring your attention to the air flowing into and out of your lungs. Notice how it passes in through your nose, into your chest and then back out through your nose or mouth.

3. Now start to take deeper, slower breaths. Bring the air down into your lungs (as far as is comfortable) so that your belly rises. Place your hand on your belly so you can feel it rise and fall.

4. Practise this deep breathing for a minute or two.

5. Now, as you inhale, hold in your mind your chosen focus word. Imagine the air flowing into your lungs carrying that sensation of relaxation with it.

6. As you exhale, imagine that the air leaving your body is carrying away the tension or anxiety.

7. Continue for as long as is comfortable. You could start by aiming for a couple of minutes and then work up to five minutes.

'Sometimes the most important thing in a whole day is the rest we take between two deep breaths.'

Etty Hellesum

YOUR HAPPY PLACE

You can use this exercise when you're feeling stressed or worried to calm your mind and help you feel relaxed.

Your happy place may be somewhere that you've visited or an entirely imagined space specifically designed just for you. It might be a place associated with happy childhood memories or a great holiday. It might be outside on a beach, or in a forest, or inside a cosy cottage. Don't forget, you can have more than one happy place.

TIP/ If you struggle to fall asleep, try this exercise to bring your mind and body into a more relaxed state.

- Find a calm and quiet place where you can sit or lie down comfortably.

- Close your eyes and focus on your breathing for a few moments. Then take a few deep breaths and allow the movement of the air in and out of your lungs to relax you.

- Once you feel relaxed, move your attention to your imagination. You are about to enter your happy place. What do you see? Maybe it's a door, or a path, or a gate, or a gap between sand dunes.

- Move through into your happy place. What can you see?

- Think about your other senses. What can you smell, hear, touch? How does the ground beneath your feet feel?

- Feel free to move around and explore the space or settle down and just enjoy the sensation of peace and safety.

- When you are ready to leave the space, bring your attention back to your breathing and, when you're ready, open your eyes.

Colour

What's your favourite colour? You probably haven't been asked that since you were twelve years old, but it's a question worth considering. Whether it's the clothes on your back or the paint on your walls, we all make choices about the colours we surround ourselves with, and colours have been shown to influence our thoughts and feelings in a variety of ways. For instance, cool blues and greens tend to be associated with feeling calm and relaxed, whereas bright oranges and yellows are more energetic and positive.

Some of these responses to colour appear to be relatively universal and are perhaps connected to our relationship with the natural world, while others are lead by culture and personal experience. For example, these days we tend to think of pink as a feminine colour and blue as masculine, but in the nineteenth century it was the other way around.

Consider now how different colours affect you. What do you personally associate with different colours? What memories do they conjure up? Imagine being surrounded by a particular colour. What feelings does it bring forward for you?

TIP/ As a relaxation exercise you could create a drawing (as
abstract and messy as you like) using different shades of
colours that you find soothing.

'There are no lines
in nature, only
areas of colour, one
against another.'

Edouard Manet

MOVE

You probably already know that exercising supports both your physical and mental wellbeing. But it's worth remembering that we don't always have to hit the treadmill or even break a sweat to benefit from this connection between our minds and bodies. Depending on how you move your body, it can help to make you feel anything from euphoric and energized to relaxed and confident or calm and focused. Just a simple walk can help us process our emotions, think through problems or unlock our creativity.

Over the next week, pay attention to how you move your body and how it impacts your mood and mental state.

For an instant mood-booster, few things come close to combining music and movement. It could be as part of a dance class, at a music festival or in your own home with the curtains closed. Turn up the volume and just let yourself go.

♪ MONDAY

♪ TUESDAY

♪ WEDNESDAY

♪ THURSDAY

♪ FRIDAY

♪ SATURDAY

♪ SUNDAY